Table of Contents

Introduction 5

Chapter 1. Inventory 7

Chapter 2. Pricing 11

Chapter 3. Marketing 16

Chapter 4. The Day of The Sale 19

Final Words 25

Thank You Page 26

Garage Sale Guide For Beginners: Garage Sales Tips to Make Quick and Easy Money by Selling Used Items

By Dale Blake

Garage Sale Guide For Beginners:

Garage Sales Tips to Make Quick and Easy Money by Selling Used Items

By

Dale Blake

Introduction

The garage sale, the yard sale, the rummage sale; it's a bit of Americana that hasn't become dated one bit. It makes just as much sense now to hold one; it's just as much fun as to attend one. Garage sales, for some, have even become a major part of a new modern enterprise called retail arbitrage. Garage sales make sense (because they make dollars). Rather than throw out your old cluttering mess, or allowing it to fester and take up space in your home, with a bit of hard work and planning, you can transform that mess into a nice little stack of bills.

Now a garage sale may not be rocket science (it isn't), but that doesn't mean that every sale is the same. If you've ever gone out bargain hunting yourself, you'll recall that there are good garage sales, and others that you wouldn't have wasted the time to walk through. We'll discuss some tips and ideas on how to attract more and more motivated buyers to your sale, how to use layout to encourage both drop-in shoppers and encourage browsing and buying, streamline setup, how to manage pricing for the biggest payoff, and a few other ideas to help you really clean up...that's the other great thing about a garage sale; in the process of making some 'free' money, you get to clean up all your old clutter and messes, by earning cash, which you can use to buy more stuff...and have another garage sale!

Chapter 1. Inventory

Well, if you want to have a garage sale, you're going to need some things to sell. This is the time to embrace the demeanor of a strict governess, or drill sergeant, or futuristic cleaning robot (whatever works for you). First, start with the big stuff. It's much easier to identify big-ticket items that you've probably been thinking of getting rid of for some time now. Finally ready to replace that old sofa? Great, write it down on an inventory list (that way it's permanent). Go through the house writing down any of the big things you want to sell. The "extra" coffee pot in the cabinet over the refrigerator, that hideous nightstand lamp that you've "gotten used to"...anything you're ready to be rid of.

Now that you had some to warm up to a no-nonsense garage sale clearance mode, it's time to go hunting for the small stuff. This can be a fun event. Get some help for this one because having someone else around will help keep you honest (recruit a friend, get the whole family involved, or have a two-house sale with your neighbor and help each other out) Everyone gets a box to go hunting with, and everyone gets assigned a territory. Then, go through everything piece by piece.

Think of the stuff in your home in one of three terms: keep, sell, trash. Try not to get stuck in the 'maybe' zone because this will just make more work for you later. Be ruthless when allowing something to remain in the 'keeper pile' (have no ruth…NONE!).

Now that you've each scavenged your own space, go through and check. Kids are great helpers, but they need helping parting with many belongings. It helps to remind them that with the money they will make, they can buy that new bicycle they want etc. It also teaches a pretty good lesson about value: both the value of money and the value of memory and sentiment (nice little bonus). But the kids aren't the only ones who may have overlooked a thing or two. Go back and be honest with yourself. If it helps, the more items you have for sale, the more people you'll attract to your garage sale, the more success the event will be. Try to get in the mood of "ooh…we can sell this thing too". Don't worry about getting carried away in this phase, because you'll have a reality check when you go through the pricing phase. Now that you're done with that, you and your partners will do the same with attics, garages, and basements. Maintain the same three point strategy of keep, sell, trash and it will simplify the process.

Get all your inventory in one place (if possible) because you're going to give it a sound once over before pricing time. Wipe everything with a cloth and a bit of cleaner, get the dead spiders out of old vases and such, dust off old wall hangings, pictures, and postcards (by the way, old pictures and postcards sell surprisingly well; as long as you don't feel creepy about a stranger taking home your old photos, then throw them in there too). Just give everything quick wipe/dust/spray, just to make it presentable. If your merchandise is clean, people will be more attracted and stay longer. The more people at your sale at any given time, the more people they'll attract...good for sales.

Some More Tips

Your garage sale doesn't need to have a theme (old furniture...kid's old toys). People love to experience the random surprises at a good sale. For that reason, sell everything. We already mentioned old photos and postcards, and that goes for posters, souvenirs, pennants, and any other memorial type item. People use them to decorate restaurants, as decorations for theme parties, or to store in their house until they have a garage sale (-maybe-). The point is, don't make judgment decisions about what is and what is not sale worthy...allow your customers to decide for themselves.

Another mistake people make; it isn't broken, it's spare parts. There are plenty of handy people out there. Heck, we're a nation of tinkerers and inventors. Broken televisions and other electronics, vacuum cleaners (HOT!)...basically anything with a motor in it, old tools, saw blades, brackets, frames...anything that an inventive mind could put to use. Sell that stuff at song, and be glad someone paid you for the privilege of hauling it away.

In general, there is someone out there to buy almost every piece of –ahem...every item in your sale. Don't hinder your own sale. So what if nine people walk by and wonder 'who would buy that', the tenth person might just walk up and show you who. Give your customers the chance to find things they want...offer them everything you've got.

Chapter 2. Pricing

Pricing can be tricky. You remember what you paid for those jeans, but used is used regardless of the quality. Many people will balk when they realize how much money they will 'lose' by selling something at a garage sale discount. There's a good rule of thumb that the pros use: If you haven't used it/worn it/ seen it/ thought about it in the last year, then it goes in the sale. You aren't losing money, because at the moment you're doing nothing more than hoarding it.

So what's a fair price? That's tricky. You want the bulk of your items to be in the $1-$5 range. This will entice browsing...and browsing (as we all know) will eventually entice buying. With your more interesting, unique, or expensive items, it will get a bit trickier. But here's a modern twist that might surprise you.

You see, many people are making a living these days by buying items at garage sales, and then selling them on the internet for very healthy profits (sometimes ten times what they paid for it). When these people go out treasure hunting, they will usually only by something if they can get at least three times their money back. They have fancy phone applications to handle on-the-spot pricing, etc. With your more interesting items, it would be worth your time to do a little homework. Go onto Ebay or Amazon FBA and search for your item. Include brand and model (if you can). Take a look at completed auctions (not open auctions). This way you'll have an idea what the item is worth to a buyer. Price the item at just below 1/3 of the average sales price. This number may seem high to you. Perhaps you were going to charge $10 for that lamp, but your math says to charge $18. Or that old iron you found in the basement, you would have been happy for $1…but your math tells you it's worth at least $12. Later we'll talk about how to bait the professional garage sale hunters to lure them in to see your high value goods.

Tagging

There are two main schools of thought when it comes to price tags; tag every item, price by box/table. I am very much in favor of one method, and one method only. You'll understand my reasoning in a moment. Place yourself at an all day garage sale (your sale if you like). It's a hit, and people are coming and going all day. They are walking up to you expectantly, with some item in their hand, in order to offer you an insultingly low number for it...all in good spirit. They wander back dejected and put it back on the table. As the day wears on, the pickins get slim. Someone walks up to buy one of the snow globes from your old collection and they hand you $1. Now you distinctly remember that all the snow globes were on the $5 table. Now you've got a dilemma. Was it moved incidentally over the course of the sale, or is something more nefarious afoot? Either way, that customer is probably going to be disappointed, and disappointed customers are no fun...and this should be as fun and easy as possible.

It's just easier when items are tagged. Use blue or tan painters tape and write the prices right on the tape. Keep your pricing simple: $0.25, $0.50, $1, $2, $5 etc. This makes it easier for the customer to tally their purchase (and look for just one more thing...) and makes the cash transaction much simpler. Try to put the tape-tag in a place where it will do no harm to the item itself. In some instances, you may have to hang a small tag from a string...just double the tape around a length of string, or a bread-bag twisty tie, and attach the tag that way.

An improvement on this tag system is the color coded sale. This makes your life easier, adds an element of fun surprise for you customers, and works great. Go to your local office supply store or craft store. Purchase colored circle stickers. You'll need about 6 colors (one for each price). Tag your merchandise with the colored dot that corresponds to the appropriate price (green = $1, red = $5etc.) The all you have to do (or have the kids do it) is make a series of pricing charts to hang all around the sale. This has an added bonus that it encourages parents to let their kids 'shop' a bit on their own. "ok, you can go find something you like with a green or a red sticker on it) That frees up mom or dad to do some shopping of their own!

Some items cannot have a tag attached either by tape, or by string. Try putting these in clear zip-lock bags and then sticking a price to the bag. Also, things like pictures, old cassette tapes, albums...anything of a certain group that you are willing to price together, can go into a box or bin. No need to label these individually. The same goes for clothing, if you are willing to price them all the same. 'Kid's clothes $2 an item'. You'd probably do better to price clothes individually, but if you have a lot of clothing to sell, you'll break even in the end and save yourself lots of time and hassle if you just price in bulk. Select items like coats, nice shoes, maternity clothes and the like can carry a separate tag and be positioned away from the other clothing at the sale.

When deciding on a price, remember that this stuff is about two days away from becoming garbage. Be realistic about what your treasures are worth. Find joy in the fact that the things you once enjoyed are going to continue on in life, with someone completely new, which is a beautiful thing. In a disposable society it's great to give some of your clutter a second life. This 'happy thought' will help you maintain your zen-like calmness amidst all the chaos and mess of preparing for and holding a garage sale...breathe in − breathe out.

Chapter 3. Marketing

To realize its maximum potential, your garage sale needs a high-end, high-tech marketing campaign. People need to know where to go and when to show up (6am-3pm...serious garage sale surfers get up early). A good place to start is in your local papers.

If your town has a local gazette, then your sale belongs in there. Run an ad for two editions (or 5 days) prior to the sale. Do the same with larger local papers. Be careful with your advertisements.   There is usually a price break where posting an ad goes from relatively cheap, to surprisingly expensive. Try to come in on the cheap side.

Get it on the net as well. Post on Craigslist.com (check it out if you're not familiar). Also there are some great garage sale search engines that are really catching on quick.   Try posting your sale on Yard Sale Search, Garage Sale Hunter, Yard Hopper, or Garage Sale Source.   Many people these days, especially the professionals (and you want them at your sale) are turning to online sources to locate their next sale. Make sure you market where the money is...get online.

At some point, while you're running around town posting ads in the local paper, you may want to check in with the police clerk. In many municipalities, a permit is required to have a yard/garage sale. It would be worth finding out, lest you get shut down by city hall.

So, you've located all the resources you want to advertise in and you're ready to write your ads. Your wording can make a huge difference. First, at the top, big letters, GARAGE SALE. Then the date(s). Then some key words to describe what you'll be selling: Clothing, Video Game eqp., Collectables, Tools, Knick-knacks. Over 300 items for sale (or whatever). If you and your neighbor are in on it together, be sure to advertise that as well with 'multi-family' or 'mutli-household'. These are the phrases that will make the professional's ears ring. Finally, close with your street address.

Just advertising the sale will bring your motley array of garage sale enthusiasts and curiosity seekers. You need targeted wording to bring the other set, the serious buyers. And our third system of marketing will help to attract the casual passerby. The old standby: Garage Sale sign...with an arrow pointing the way.

Seriously, if you want casual curious people to stop by on a Saturday morning, this is all you need. GARAGE SALE ....Bold Black lettering, nothing fancy

DATE.........................Don't   write   the   word today...actually write the date

----->..................... And put an arrow pointing them in the right direction.

Kids are great for making garage sale signs, but you can do it too. Remember light background, bold black print...keep it simple. Use white, yellow, or neon green poster board and big black permanent marker. Letter as large as you can fit on the poster. Make a bunch, thirty or forty if there are several main roads in your area. Draw a half-mile circle around your house and post signs from all directions leading to your sale. This ensures that not only do the neighbors know, but that anyone passing through the area in any direction will see at least one of your signs. (again, check with local regulations, it may not be legal to post unapproved signs). Oh, and make sure you get signs facing in both directions on those outer main roads, you want to snag everyone you can.

Chapter 4. The Day of The Sale

You've been working hard, but you're not done yet (in fact the sale hasn't even started). The first thing you'll do is set up your tables (you did remember that you need lots and lots of tables right?) Folding tables, card tables, any table is good. Lengths of board over cinder block can be used to make very pleasant shelves. Plywood over sawhorses is great. The point is, your creativity in creating tables will better showcase your wares, and appeal to the typical garage sale hunter's sense of esthetique absurd. Beg, borrow, and steal (ok don't steal) any flat surface you can find and prop it up on something. Tabling your wares is absolutely non-negotiable. Now, some things: hot wheels cars $1 each —they can go in a bin. Assorted sports balls...sure they can all go together. But it's a mistake to assume that people will want to paw through baskets of clothing, or even dig through piles of books. Think about when you go to a store and the experience you want to have.

Think of It as a Store

Just for today, you are transforming your front yard into a place of business; what kind of business do you run? Think about the logistics and flow of the sale itself. You want to encourage fluid movement into the sale, and then create a smaller escape point at the far end of the browsing line. You want people to move freely, and to be able to access the goods from more than one direction. One good layout is tables along the outside with a table or clothing rack in the center. This creates a horseshoe effect where the customer is surrounded by goods wherever they go. This is a rich and engaging environment.

Lure them in with some of the larger items near the road. A sofa, a foosball table, maybe a piece of exercise equipment. Give them something big so they know they're at the right place. Of course the old balloons tied to a mailbox always does the trick as well.

Segregate and distribute your merchandise. This is another benefit to tagging your wares rather than using table-pricing. You can put all your kitchen stuff together even if they are different prices. Same with decorations, furnishings, toys, baby items, outdoor gear, tools. Think of the stores you go to. They don't have everything all mish-mashed up. Neither should you. The goal is to get every single guest to take a look at every single item. That gives you the best odds of making sales.

Display your clothing. If you don't have a standing clothing rack (and you can't borrow one) improvise one. Clothes sell better when they're hanging up. You can probably borrow (or get free) a whole bunch of hangers from a local drycleaner or thrift shop. String a clothesline between two trees or two buildings. Hang them from your garage door. The point is, create a clothing section and display the clothing. Think of your home as a second hand shop for the day. Some people even create a space where customers can try something on...the more creative you are with creating a store-like atmosphere, the more engaged your guests will be.

Also, don't neglect their needs. Run an extension cord out to the sale so buyers can test electronics. Have some batteries on hand for the same purpose (sorry batteries not included...or you can buy some cheap bulk batteries and sell them as well). Have lots and lots of plastic shopping bags on hand. You are buried in them anyway, why not store up a bunch so people can carry off their wares. Likewise, save up or collect newspaper to wrap up the breakables. If possible, prepare a bathroom for strangers. Clean up personal effects, remove any valuables, put out your 'not the best' hand towels. Put down some extra floor mats between the entrance and the commode. Probably more than one person will ask, and you may as well accommodate.

Create Atmosphere

Who says it has to be weird to have a bunch of strangers pawing through your stuff while loitering on your front lawn and abusively haggling over a quarter off the price of a used egg-beater...it doesn't have to be weird. You can create ambience at your sale as much for the clients enjoyment as for your own peace of mind. For yourself, make it an event. If you think of it as a trial to endure, you'll hate it. C'mon, you're outside, decluttering your home, meeting new (and strange) people, and making money at the same time. In that spirit, get some tunes going.

This is also a great time for your neighbor to sell her famous cookies, for the kids to sell lemonade, or to just have a cooler of juice boxes and bottled water (for sale of for free). It all goes to creating a welcoming pleasant space where people linger...remember, people are like pigeons. If they see one doing something, they'll come just to investigate. It pays to keep people around.

One way to encourage more browsing is to intersperse your highest quality items throughout the sale. It really doesn't even matter if they fit the theme of that section. People will continue through the whole sale just to see what else you have. For this reason, it pays to have a few 'show pieces'.

Haggling

People will want to haggle. They will want a nickel off that broken tea saucer, or a dollar-twenty five off that $30 bicycle. Stay calm and remain pleasant. For the first few hours just tell people that everything is priced as marked. Invite them to return near the end of the sale to haggle on any remaining goods (this is a great way to unload unsold items) Don't be tempted to take the first offer you get early in the sale. If you did your marketing right, then trust that people are on their way. Wait until ten or noon to start bargaining with people, unless you enjoy the game. With those specialty items that you price checked on the internet, you may want to create a bargain hunter section. This way the professionals can go right for the meat of the sale. Your casual seekers may scoff at your pricing on those items, but you'll know a pro right away when they beeline for that table, and then head straight to you to make offers on the whole collection.

What's Left

Most likely you aren't going to sell everything at your garage sale. Don't just lug it back into the house so it can go back to taking up space. Throw all the little stuff in a box, put it out to the curb and mark it FREE. With items in good quality, you can take them to a thrift store. Or better yet, donate them to a local charity. You get a receipt for the full purchase price which you can then use to write off a piece of your taxes. You see, it all has a purpose, and it ALL MUST GO.

Final Words

A well organized, well marketed, well run garage sale can be pleasant, fun, and profitable. It can help you clear out the clutter, and be a refreshing exercise in want versus need. You can use it as a learning opportunity for the young ones, and a chance to connect with neighbors again. The keys to minimizing stress and maximizing earnings are planning and preparation. Fridays and Saturdays are best, and try avoid the midsummer's heat.

Garage sales are a part of our history, a part of our present, and they represent the entrepreneurial side of the American 'Can Do' spirit. If you organize you time, and your belongings, and go through the process step-by-step, then you 'can do' it too. So grab some boxes and start digging. You'll be amazed how fast that trash turns to treasure and how piles of dusty junk turn into piles bills. Plus you'll reclaim your own home from decades of accumulation, and that is priceless.

I want to personally thank you for reading my book. I hope you found information in this book useful and I would be very grateful if you could leave your honest review about this book. I certainly want to thank you in advance for doing this.

If you have the time, you can check my other books too.